LISTEN TO ME:
A COLLECTION OF POETRY AND PROSE

LISTEN TO ME:
A COLLECTION OF POETRY AND PROSE

Written By: Dmitra-Dejahnae Lucas

Illustration/Book Design By: Ra Brown

Listen to Me: A Collection of Poetry and Prose
© 2022 Dmitra-Dejahnae Lucas
ISBN: 978-0-578-35908-3

First Edition, 2022

Printed in the United States of America

Illustration/Book Design by Ra Brown
Layout by Emily Anne Evans

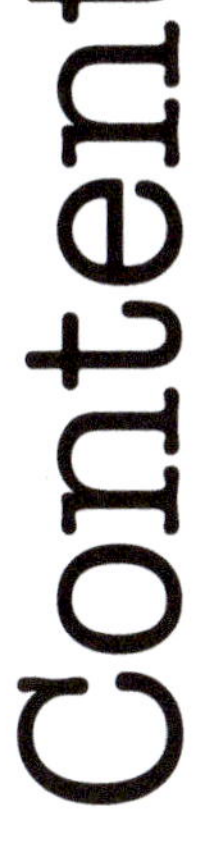

Contents

YOU ARE WHO YOU SAY YOU ARE
YOUR WORDS CAST SPELLS YOU
HAVE MORE PO... IN YOU THAN
YOU KNOW B...UL OF YOUR
CHOSEN ...CAUSE YOU
WILL RE... YOU THINK
SAY AND ... SLIGHTEST
WHISPER ... DEAR YOUNG
LIFE ... HASTE
DECISIO... ...IFE PUT
DOWN THA... ...IFE DON'T TAKE
THAT CH... O...YOUR LIFE
SIT DOWN LIS...N ...W YOU
FROWN THA...S OKAY T...
OKAY THAT'S THE HUM...

1. Talking To Children

Dear Young Life

You are who you say you are
Your words cast spells
You have more power in you than you know
Be careful of your chosen words because you will reap those
you think, say, and even the slightest whisper will sow
Dear young life, don't make haste decisions under strife
Put down that knife.
Don't take that chance on your life.
Sit down. Listen now.
You can frown.
That's okay.
That's the human in you that they try to strip away.
Feel what you feel. Feel it all. Let it all out.
If you ever need an ear, call on me.
I'll hear you out.
Take a deep breath.
Wipe your face, pick up your head.
Go at your own pace, life is not a race.

Kujichagulia : Self-Determination

Tests don't define you
Label you, criticize you
They won't demise you

Embrace who you are
Head held down only to draw
Scream, spell, pronounce your name

You have everything
to gain, reclaim; welcome in
peace, love, self-determination

2. Talking To Friends

# Friend in you

Please be there for me
When I don't ask. I pray
Friends are what we stay

Going to the sun

Fly to it with your
Wings you've grown from releasing
The pain from your past

ACCEPTANCE

Authentically
Cultivating
Compassionate and
Ever-lasting bonds
Prioritizing what I set my efforts to,
Transcending old habits and emotional guards
Allowing myself to give love and receive love
Never taking the time I have (with someone) for granted
Channeling my own personal power(s)
Essentially trusting my pace in the world

3. Talking To Love Interests

Listen to me

Listen to me.
Listen to me for understanding.
Understand what I mean when I say, and even what I mean when I may say different.
Understand the message, the feelings in between my lines.
Understand where I'm comin' from to help you understand where it is I'm goin.
Understand that my words tell no lies.
Understand that I'm already knowin' I got bold, razor blade slick wit' it sass.
Listen to me when I'm mad.
Listen to me yell, listen to me shout, listen to me tell you how it is.
What it ain't.
And let's work on what it's gon' be.

Star Struck

His lips the vinyl
As his tongue moves
to the tune and bass
his voice sings the soundtrack

His lethal hands don't need gloves
They offer love and exude white light
A hand held sends neurologic reactions
to erupt my San Andreas fault

His ideologies depict my deepest fantasies
Both in the world and in my mind
He runs away to my dreams at night
I astral-project into his realities

Still Ascending

He says he likes my intellect.
My mind ain't in its prime
And he doesn't even know it yet
Doesn't know I still speak with a colonized tongue
Because the sway of my hips
Rhythm in my steps
notes of my tumbao are so indigenously sung

He says he likes my intellect
Lets see if I can make him sweat
Put him to the test because
That is the institutionalized way to measure the return of a
human being
as I challenge his ways of thinking
Does he give brain like he went to college?
I mean
Does he possess unknown knowledge?
And is he dedicated enough to actually apply it
How does he view the world?

He says he likes my intellect
Legs stretched out and head cocked back
as we gaze upon the stars
Passing back and forth theories, histories and conspiracies
He inhales I exhale
While hazy clouds form
Polluting even more the colonized sky above us

He says he likes my intellect
Well he don't even know that I'm still ascending

4. Talking To Family

(Felt like) My father's only child

Dad, our relationship has grown most within my years of adulthood. I've come to know more about you than I've asked, just as you've come to know the real adult me. I'm grateful to still have you with me, to be able to learn from your knowledge and your mistakes, to be able to have had a father-daughter relationship, that I have memories of you since birth, that you're still able. I pray our relationship continues to stay rooted in the trails of our ancestors and stem through the concrete of misunderstandings, generational gaps and bud, blossom and then bloom from June to June

1/3

Your laugh sets off a chain of fireworks.
Light exudes from your smile, your style and the way you
move to the melody
Beat your lowest self and rebuilt, reformed and rebranded
who others knew as Deedee
It was your gray, saddened days you never let your oldest
daughter see
Thats why your drive, get up n go, dance to your own beat
fiery light was reincarnated and lives within she.
She is me, one of your three

My brother's current keeper

Did he show himself love today?
I mean really show himself love today
Wash off reality, breath in, and meditate
Stone walled resorts sheds no light on recidivism
No it don't lead the way

Did he show himself love today?
I mean really show himself love today
Wash off reality, breath in, and meditate
Personal drug dealers
Big booty property guards
What do they really keep away?
Did he show himself love today?

Commissary buffets
Reeses, kitkat, hot cocoa you don't get back
 and 10 cups of noodles a day

Did he get to see the day?
I mean actually kiss the sun today
Stone walled resorts sheds no light on recidivism
No it don't lead the way

Two cent per minute calls comin my way
Did he know I thought of him today?
He crosses my mind like everyday
Sometimes I answer, only afford to hear his name

Im red, he's blue
One sperm, two wombs
He motivates me to lead the way

Did he get to see the day?
I mean actually kiss the sun today?
Stone walled resorts sheds no light on recidivism
No it don't lead the way

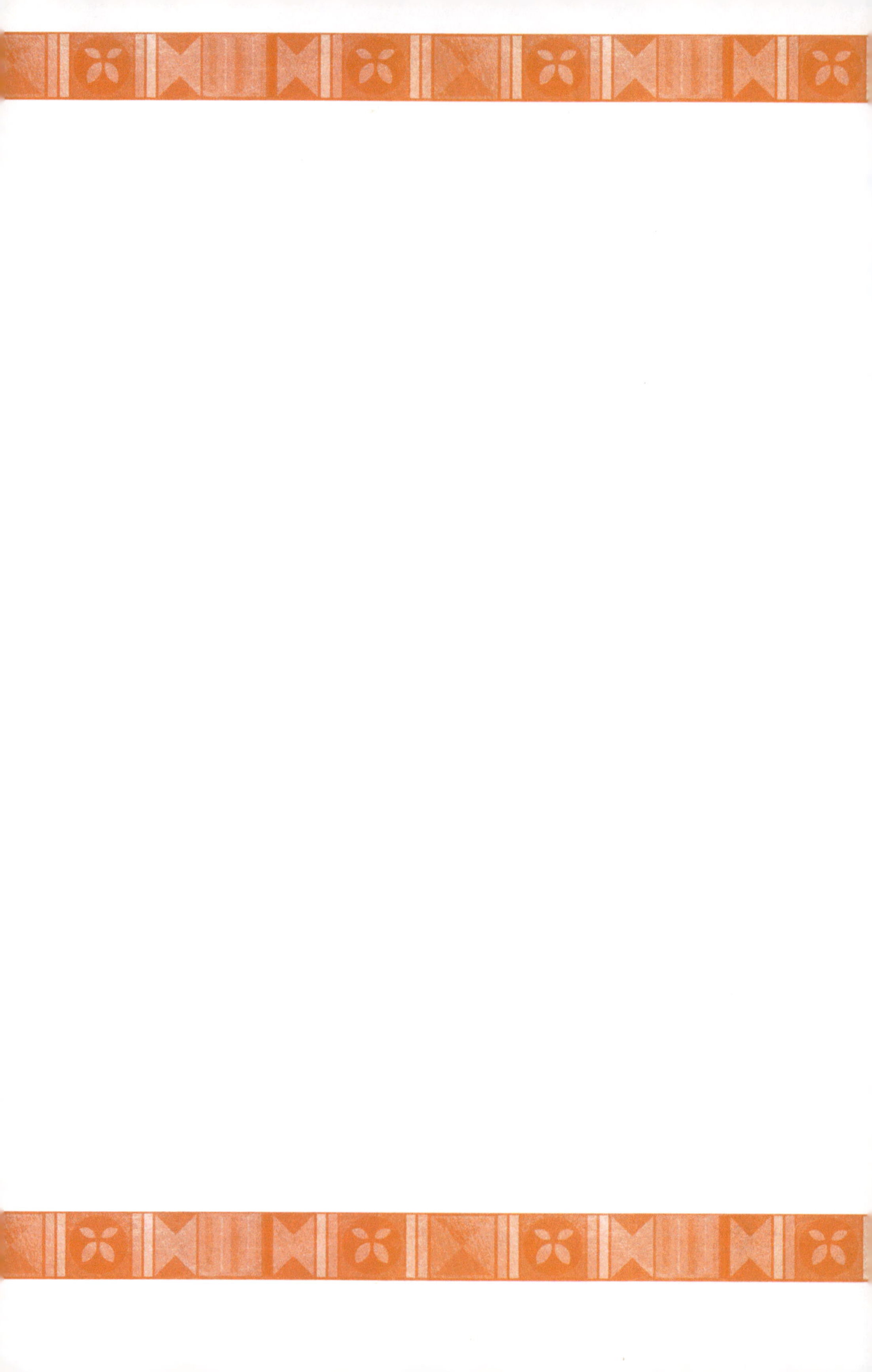

T WAS ME WANTING HIM TO BE
WITH ME IT WAS ME WANTING
HIM TO BE WHAT I DIDNT HAVE
T WAS ME WANTING HIM TO BE
WHAT HE DID NOT WANT TO BE
T WAS ME ________ING HIM TO BE
______ ______ ______ WHO B____OR
ALTHOUG______ ________ ____NOT HIM
T WAS ME ____________ ________ B_
SOM____
T WAS _______
THER____

5. Talking To Self

DMITRA

Dedicated continuing after your dreams even while drowning in feelings of defeat
The amount of grit within you is magnanimous
Before the institutional walls confined your imagination you were always infinitely intelligent, imaginative
Tenacious in the pursuit of you. Exploring every alley and avenue
Revitalizing old ways, refining your image to reform the you that they tried to run into the ground. Burry you like a seed yet you stayed rooted
You are amazing, amable, able and astoundingly attractive.

I Am the House

I got bold, razor blade slick wit it sass
I don't need no pvc or copper pipe brass
Built up brick by brick.
Firefighter red,
Eye catcher, walls laid with giraffe print
Dream catcher, actualizer, everything is meant

I got bold, razor blade slick wit it sass
My walk, my talk, twinkling shards of glass
Candied apple, mouth waterin', stickin to ya teeth
Savory oil poppin', get into the crisp meat
Critical, greater than the physical,
fencing eurocentric heteronormativity to demise
Drowning oceans, head butting stampedes, roller coastin'
naked on sherbet skies

I got bold, razor blade slick wit is sass
Firecracker, my spark warms souls without gas
Foresee treasures, thrones and progression
Fuck my anatomy Im a walkin erection
Drippin of all seven seas
Experiencing more knowledge than can be taught from those
with degrees

Hierarchy of Needs

All my ex's like the music that catch the youngins taste
That's probably why they was only temporary
Only willing to hold me down so I didn't blow away
But couldn't lift me up, motivate me thats why its only dreams
I chase
Got caught up in a rat race for cheese n shelter
Aint know that physiological needs is only the base
Chillin in comfort, yet nothin' changes so in the corner's
compiles waste
Wasted space in their heart, their mind and damn near in their
soul
I want to raise kids but only kids of my own, don't got no time
to be raisin the one I made one with
We ain't seein' eye to eye and thats cus you eye level to my
clit
I'm so tall, I'm a giant, I see way so far above you, my head up
in the clouds
Forseein property, healthy livin', and a sense of connection
I'm thankin' God and countin up all of my blessings
That I'm free from the chains, rangs and glittery possessions
I got self-respect, esteem, and awareness. I don't have to
purchase it
Actualizing the words I said back when with them.
I guess separating from that path helped me to see
retrospectively
Who I desire, aspire; to bring out what's within.
Can't shrink myself no mo just to fit in.
Im gon' be the most I can be
No more letting them dim what's within

My Heaux Tales

It was me wanting him to be with me
It was me wanting him to be what I didn't have
It was me wanting him to be what he did not want to be
It was me wanting him to be the man he could not be for me
It was me wanting him to be him because I missed him
although he was not him
It was me wanting him to be something I needed
It was me wanting him to be there for me
It was me wanting him to be there for me when he couldn't
even be there for himself
It was me wanting him
It was me wanting
It was me

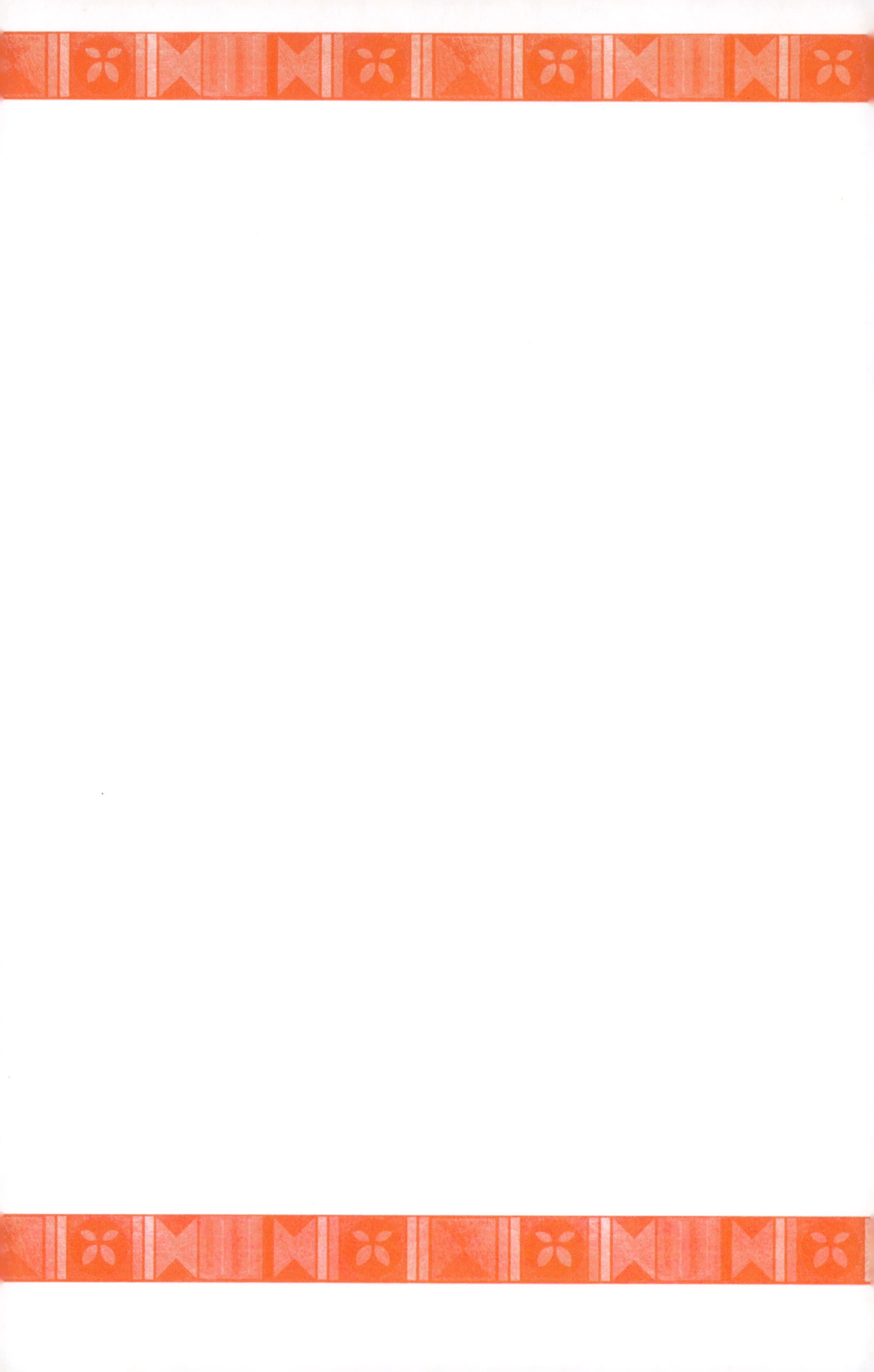

6. Talking To Ancestors

The sun and the moon

You're the flame in the
middle of someone's day and
you light their dark nights

CAPITALISM

It was all foreseen
The history and hustle with money
Earnin' it then spendin it times three
It wont let me free
Been chasing it since a teen
Traveled overseas
Even got degree'd
Still can't seem to get free
J.O.B yeah I keep 2 to 3
The system's got a hold of me
Is it really all it seems?
VVS, VVs and Louie Vs
Dust collecting things
Leave you blind trying, buying and eating things
You might as well be injecting yourself with disease
Remember everything you do
and don't do
is passed down thru the
Stems, bark and roots of your family tree

Untitled PT 1:

Perished from the physical
Yet we feel you float throughout
now all there is is your spiritual

Images of head shakin' and Taka drippin' down the spout
Turned to it as often as U-turns made around Highway 12
Choice turned into habit, turned lifestyle into cold casket

Drowned at the bottom
Only surfacing to gasp for air and
exhale the heated C2H6O vapors that charged your battery
Even AA can't break plastic bottles sealed with blue caps
Nor cure the generational curses of African men made in
America

Untitled PT 2:

The smell of liquor lingered
Taunted and tickled my cilia
Inflated my lungs
Like the burned food forgotten at the bottom of the stove
Stone and cemented in my tracks
As the reminiscent train flew by
Alerted olfaction
And carried the redolence that
rattled the chains of my memories
Images on 35mm film rolling down hill
Eroding good times, chafing and chipping them away with
each

"Shut Up"
"Shut Up"
"Shut the fuck up"
"SHUT THE FUCK UP"

Is what I tell my screams
They wake me up at night
Just as your hollerin' over
Mad TV
Mad due to the tv
did through hollow loft walls

"Shut Up"
"Shut Up"
"Shut the fuck up"
"SHUT THE FUCK UP"

Is what I say to the repeated abuse
replaying.
repeating.
retraumatizing.
reopening mental wounds.
A reintroduction of all the hidden records
That rewound time
To remind us that even in our dreams we are not safe

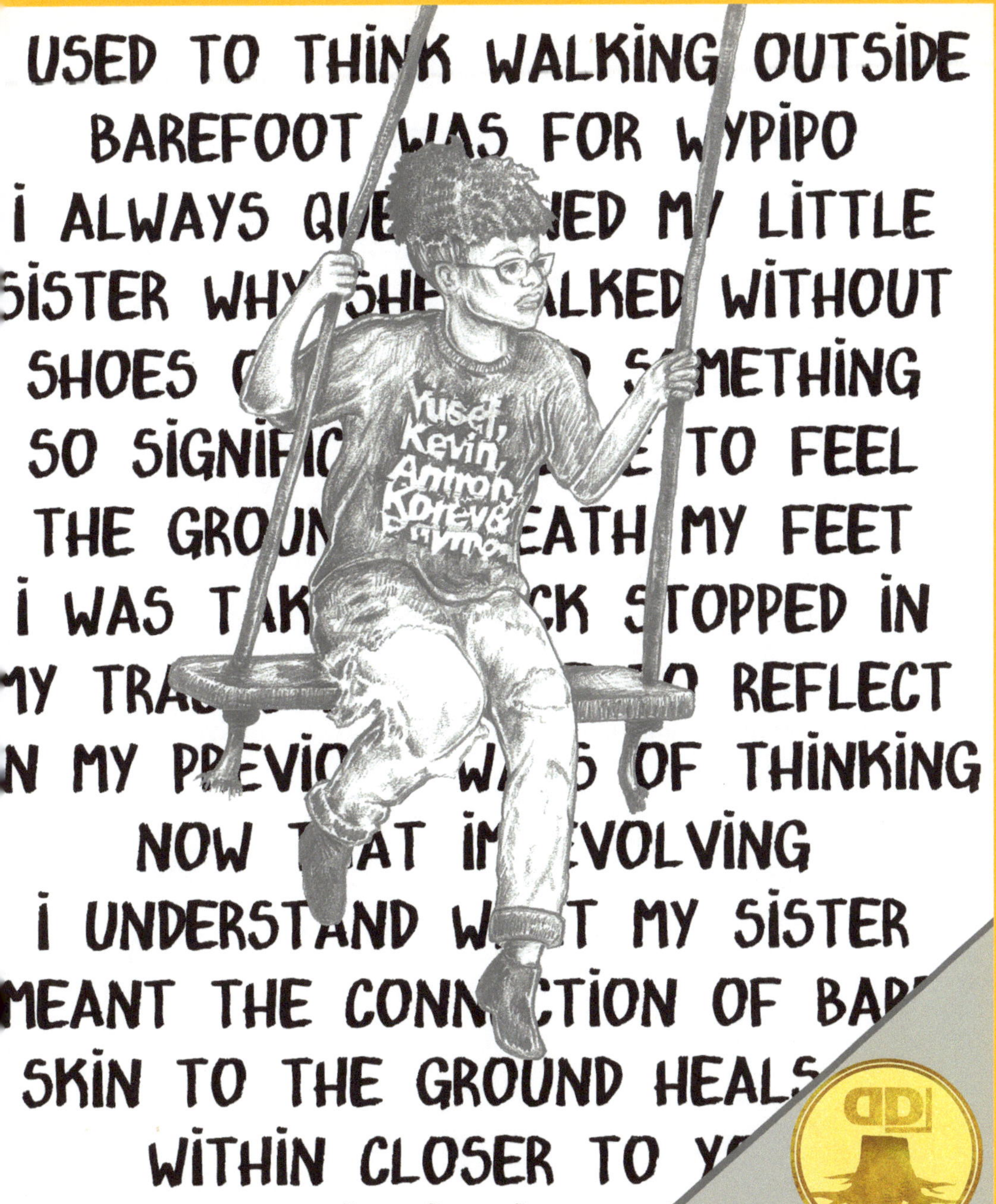

7. Talking To God

It's called the ground for a reason

I used to think walking outside barefoot was for wypipo.
I always questioned my little sister why she walked outside
without shoes on
It wasn't until one day she responded
And said something so significant
"I like to feel the ground beneath my feet"
I was taken aback, stopped in my tracks and made to reflect
on my previous ways of thinking
Now that I'm evolving I understand what my sister meant
The connection of bare skin to the ground heals us within
Closer to YOU, closer to what's within
I now walk on the grass in my backyard with no shoes, socks
or sandals.
I call on my ancestors and YOU to ground myself
Connect myself with life, with the land I live on, survive from
and come from.
I am the land, soil, dirt, grass and sand
It holds me in its hand
I am rooted. I am connected. I am safe. I am taken care of. I
am grounded.

kNOw History, kNOw Self

Heart breaking we do not know the names of your children,
sons, and daughters yet we know the tales to their end
Eyes wander to the back of my hippocampus as I try to recall
the soul she is speaking of by name
How infernal
How hegemonic of ameriKKKa to paint the colors of our lives
as one to erase what glows within
They paint "Black Lives Matter" to forget where the bodies
spilt blood
How rude of me to demand another pronounce my syllables
correctly
While I cannot recall all the names of the lives I chant matter.
Only the ones the crows plucked and prodded to be the faces
of 400 plus years on repeat
How eurocentric
How hegemonic of ameriKKKa to paint the colors of our lives
as one to erase what glows within
Heartbreaking we do not know the names of all your children
yet we know the tales to their end
They get blown by the wind daily because like leaves there
are too many to gather

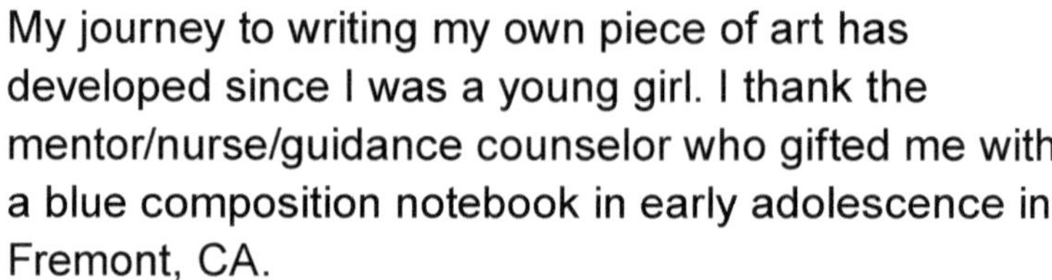

Acknowledges, Accolades and Applauds

My journey to writing my own piece of art has developed since I was a young girl. I thank the mentor/nurse/guidance counselor who gifted me with a blue composition notebook in early adolescence in Fremont, CA.

I thank my father on Earth, in the flesh, Dmitri Julian Lucas, who patiently, intentionally and persistently helps lead me to our Father in the sky and Heavens above. Without your act and part in creation, I would not be here.

I thank the Black men who helped me curate my first Black piece of written art. These names below served as inspiration to write poetry, with intent to fuel and pull emotions from my inner mind, body and spirit to share with the world.

The Entrepreneur Che" also known as
(LIL C - That One Nigga);

>without the work you put in for yourself I would not
have had the skeleton, the blueprint to pursue this
path to becoming a self-published author on her
way to making a lot of money publishing books.

Ra Brown;

>without our first initial conversation at Lake Merritt in
Oakland, CA I would not have had a Black man of
your talent, graciousness and academic excellence
in graphic design commit to seeing my ideas be
drawn to fruition.

Chef Beanz;

>without your presence on social media I would
not have questioned my own thoughts, actions,
conversations, and patterns and how they played
parts to me living without mindful intention.

Edward Ellis II;

>your support, friendship and own experiences of
becoming an author continue to inspire me and
serve as an example of Black folk monetizing their
passions

Set the Versifier QKA Struggle The Solo;

>your part in the creation of HER: Heaven's Epitome
Realized and the artistry you embody inspires me to
continue developing my own.

About the Author

"[She has] everything to be iconic"

"Lethal Lucas talent"

"Relatable, powerful and captivating"

Dmitra Lucas, Fairfield, CA native, takes her first leap to deconstructing the wounded patriarchal narrative of "women are supposed to be seen and not heard" with *Listen to Me: A Collection of Poetry and Prose*. Being handed a blue composition notebook in a child's psychiatric hospital ignited Ms. Lucas' pen(wo)manship. *Listen to Me: A Collection of Poetry and Prose* is an ode to everyone surviving with blocked and unbalanced throat chakras. Ms. Lucas aims to inspire others to introspectively recognize and be true to their voice. Currently, Ms. Lucas resides in Austin, TX and manifests everything her inner child dreamed of with *Listen to Me* being the gunshot to commence her marathon.